RECALCITRANT VERSE

Nothing is quite what it seems

Tony Josolyne

Grosvenor House
Publishing Limited

This book is published by
Grosvenor House Publishing Ltd
Link House
140 The Broadway, Tolworth, Surrey, KT6 7HT.
www.grosvenorhousepublishing.co.uk

A CIP record for this book
is available from the British Library

ISBN 978-1-80381-644-9

This book is dedicated to:

Joanna and all of our family.
Also
My sister Beryl and all of her family.

CONTENTS

Foreword

Tony Josolyne's short book of poetry, 'Recalcitrant Verse: Nothing is quite what it seems' is an apt title. On the surface many of the poems are deceptively easy to read and understand, but so many of them have a hidden depth that will strike a familiar chord with readers, causing them to chuckle as in the poem, 'Grandfather's Beard,' or to reflect on the whole business of neutrality when reading 'Conforming' or to empathise with the poet's personal experience in the poem, 'Wallasey 1941'. The poems are an eclectic mix, written over several years with verses covering many different moods.

I first became aware of Tony's work when he sent a sample of his poems to Arts Richmond for their 'Poem A Day' website initiative. All of his poems were accepted and read and appreciated by a large on-line audience. I continued to follow Tony's poetry appearances at various poetry open mic gatherings. A number of his poems have also been presented at larger poetry events, including World War Remembance concerts and more recently, 'Cry Freedom', a theatrical experience that explored the concept of freedom through poetry, prose and music.

I am aware of the school of thought that a poem should stand on its own and does not need any description to explain what it is about. Normally, I would go along with this viewpoint, but in Tony's case his asides make for interesting reading as very often they provide a context and his reason for writing a particular poem. His prompts vary from personal experience as in the poem 'Travel Insurance' or his poetic response to a newspaper clipping, for example the poem, 'Cover'.

This collection of poems by Tony Josolyne is full of humour, poignancy and strong observational insights. It contains poems that are reminiscent of poems that one has heard in childhood but with a delightfully innovative twist. There are wonderful examples of parody, as in the poem 'Food for Thought' and also poems that reveal Tony's strong technical background as in 'Commerce and Technology'. This is a book of poems that will grace anybody's books of poetry shelf.

Anne Havell-Warrington
(Writer, Reviewer & founder of Poetry Performance)

Preface

During schooldays, an English schoolmaster once wrote the following comment to an early poetry attempt: "Form and description O.K. but the poem fails to give any message." Since then, I have made sure that my poems do carry some sort of message. Life is full of anomalies, I find it more rewarding to write about these, rather than generating self-obvious platitudes and poetic metaphors.

A friend, mentor and leader of a Poetry Group, once classed my poems as 'recalcitrant'. This may have been because many of them highlighted certain oddities of life; rather than being restricted by more mundane ideas.

Some newspaper reports provide fresh material of interest; however, the given information is sometimes too limited. In fairness, some news details may have to be withheld until they can be revealed openly, in the law-courts. However, personal information about victims and uncharged suspects is sometimes revealed too soon and too freely; with serious consequences.

The situations and ideas that follow come from a variety of sources, some from personal experience others from unusual news reports. Additional notes (in italics) will follow some poems. The poems do not follow any particular time sequence, some date back many years, covering news or situations current at that time; others resurrect some personal memories.

Introduction

I have included one poem from my schooldays, 'The Graveyard', because it has a personal, historic significance. Other poems from this period have been consigned to the rubbish bin.

Following an English-class coverage of Thomas Gray's 'Elegy Written in a Country Churchyard', the following homework was set: 'Compose a short poem in the style of Thomas Gray.' For some reason I kept my attempt. Some years later, I showed it to a poet friend, without telling him about its background; he deduced that I must have been been very depressed when I composed it. To me it had just been another homework, 'the creation of a poem to a set theme.' My mood at the time of writing did not seem particularly relevant. Sometime later, this friend introduced me to a local Poetry Group that he attended. I found the group to be very friendly and helpful.

Although I am moved by inconsistencies, the poems that follow will be unlikely to indicate my full state of mind at the time of composition; because they may have taken several days to complete. However, changing ideas and technology may well have had some effect on their presentation.

A School Homework Poem

The Graveyard

At daybreak, shrouds of blackness leave the field;
A chorus of crickets sings, the bees hum
And the farmer surveys his yield;
But members of the cemetery lie dumb.

There, the many stones, of different hue,
Show where decaying bones most gravely lie
And flowers, glistening with dew,
The haunting spirits of the dead defy.

But the flowers, so colourful and gay,
Mourners' flowers that made the graves so bright,
Even these in the end decay
To moulder on the ground by day and night.

There they lie among the crumbling stones
(With memories and epitaphs thereon)
Rotting, just like the buried bones,
With fading colours, all their splendour gone.

Composed for a school homework, many years ago.

Human Behaviour

Grandfather's Beard

'What a long, white beard you have, Grandad,
It flows right down to reach your chest'
'That's because I've never shaved,' he said
'It keeps me warm, without a vest.'

'Where do you keep it while you sleep,
Is it between the sheets or out?'
The old man pondered long and deep:
Then shook his aging head, in doubt:

'I really cannot answer that,
I just do what comes naturally,
Then making sure it's lying flat
I go to sleep unthinkingly.'

When he retired to bed that night,
He thought how he should place his beard:
Inside the sheets it seemed too tight,
'Might choke me while I sleep' he feared.

But when he laid his beard outside,
The quilt chafed roughly round his throat;
In and out with his beard he tried,
Until his mind began to float.

Early next morning, he awoke,
And looked around his rumpled bed:
'I know!' Excitedly he spoke…
Then suddenly… he dropped down dead.

Based on a dark tale remembered from childhood.

World Performance

A world-stage

Life's drama builds up year by year
Set scenes are often overcast
Some plots humorous, some austere
Each coming from a simple past.

Roles we take on the stage of life
Need dedication for each part:
Be it a husband, child or wife,
True feeling must come from the heart.

Throughout our lives upon this earth
We face fresh challenges each year
our human race may prove its worth
For all the aeons we live here.

From family connections in the theatre world, and current worries of growing pollution and "Global warming".

Shakespeare likened the world to a stage. In the theatre we appreciate and enjoy regular, consistent performances, but the world is continually developing, changing and challenging our way of life.

The stage-curtain of our world may come down some time in the future. Meanwhile, we try to adapt to the present and pay heed to predictions of the changes ahead.

The Law

Law Enforcement

Speaking an ill-chosen word
may be slanderous in law,
though such convictions seem absurd
prosecutions can be sure.

For violent crimes with knife and gun
the Defence Teams pull ahead:
finding proof 's not easily done
when the victims end up dead.

The law can punish minor slips of the tongue, made in jest or anger; sometimes this may lead to a successful lawsuit against the perpetrator. Through lack of evidence and independent witnesses, some street killings remain unresolved.

Only reasonable force is acceptable, when guarding your home.

Reasonable Force

'You claim,' the prosecution said,
'There was minimum use of force,
But your intruder was found dead,
From injuries of unknown source.

He suffered fractures to his skull,
Carotid artery was torn,
His state was indescribable...
He lay contorted on your lawn.

Can you tell the court the reason
For the violence he's sustained?
The signs of strangulation
Must also be explained.'

    ''I opened up a bedroom door
    And saw the burglar standing there:
    So quickly stepped across the floor
    And threw my daughter's teddy bear.

    Retreating, from this mild attack,
    He stepped upon a gift to Jane:
    The skateboard tipped, then threw him back,
    To crash right through the window pane.

    With curtain cord around his neck
    And cut by the splintering glass,
    He was a bleeding choking wreck,
    Before he landed on the grass.'

Warfare

Drake's Pride

'Your majesty, I bear good news!'
> 'Wait! We would have respect from you,
> You can't just enter when you choose,
> Get on your knees and kiss my shoe.'

'I humbly beg forgiveness,
Today's intrusion I regret,
I must approach you nonetheless,
Despite my breach of etiquette;'

> 'Then rise Sir Francis, have your say,
> I've heard news from a different source...'

'The Spanish fleet came yesterday,
Two hundred ships... a mighty force...'

> 'Yet you continued playing bowls...
> My orders for attack... defied!'

'We only had a few more *rolls*,
Our fleet was waiting... for the tide.'

> 'According to reports I've had
> Your battle didn't go too well...'

'The weather was extremely bad
Our lighter vessels went through hell.'

Continued...

Drake's Pride continued…

'I'm told our losses were too high…
For victory we had no hope'
'Whatever strategy we'd try
Our smaller ships, just couldn't cope.'

'Come to the point, no more excuses,
Just now you claimed your news was good…'
'Well… the fire-ships had their uses,
Also, their fleet ran short of food,

Their defence broken; morale gone…
A famous victory… …for us!'
'No thanks to you we beat the Don,
the outcome was fortuitous.'

Imaginary conversation between Francis Drake and Queen Elizabeth 1st with some lesser known, historic details.

Wallasey 1941

Woken up! It isn't morning yet.
Persuaded firmly, but gently from my bed;
Why does that familiar tuneless whine
Seem more ominous tonight?

Excitement kills my drowsiness
All thoughts of sleep have gone.

Four of us sit below the stairs,
Closed in, squashed together,
Hoping for protection… so they say.

I hear a distant, urgent hum,
Then sharp sporadic cracks,
And a rolling grumble, like thunder,
I can't see the 'lightning',
There's no window in our hidey-hole,
Where we sit and wait…

They try to put me at my ease
with silly jokes and childish chat.
Their faces, greyly lit
by a flickering candle,
are lined and strained,
I sense their fear.

Continued…

Wallasey 1941 continued…

Closer and louder,
now I feel the rumbling walls,
the sound is everywhere:
whistling, booming, banging, crashing
and that perpetual drone.

The foundations tremble,
our ears, deafened by the noise,
barely hear the tinkling glass;
heads are bowed in prayer.

During WW2. Much has been made of the terrible effects of London blitzes. Many other major British cities and ports (and their surrounding towns) suffered similar attacks.

From memory, this recalls my personal, childhood experience of such a blitz during a long stay with my grandparents, in Wallasey (on the outskirts of Liverpool and Birkenhead).

Lost Sounds

Time and distance shield me
from cries of inhumanity and pain;
far from sight, un-noticed,
they fade across the miles;
in distant outskirts of the world,
ignored but unsuppressed.

The media present
scant glimpses of the truth,
stark images hit the screen
but the screams are muted out.

True suffering is not appreciated when the real sounds are hidden

Armorial

Arm,
underarm, overarm
armour, arms,
armoury,
army, armada,
armistice, disarm;
re-arm, armaments...
Armageddon

Experimental: - Constructed from chosen words including the word 'arm'. the end result, unexpectedly, took on the shape of a WW2 bomb.

Cover

He prepared for Armageddon:
A stronghold underground,
A refuge with his wife and son,
Somewhere to keep them safe and sound.

They stocked up with tins and water,
And fuel, for generator power;
There were shelves of reading matter,
That would fill in many an hour.

For their comfort and their safety
There was nothing left to chance...
And when it came... that fateful day,
He gave the paper-work a glance.

Service was guaranteed for years,
Instant response to any fault!
The warranty allayed his fears -
Secure, within a private vault...

Inspired by a 2011 newspaper reporting that the Vivos website was saying that some believed that the world would end on 21st December 2012. There had been a race against time for the completion of a global network of shelters. Fortunately, December 21, 2012 passed without any major incident. If the worst had happened how valid would a warranty have been?

Contest

No buildings grace this chequered field of war,
lifeless pieces, assembled in their ranks,
are soon moved forward, through a battle-door,
without the help of missiles planes or tanks.

The players strive for personal success -
the will to win, without a gun or sword
their gambits won't put families under stress,
a king that falls can rest upon the board.

Game over... the squares are cleared again;
now self-assured, the victor leaves the room
to help confer on Russia's war campaign,
without a thought for all those facing doom.

Inspired by the USSR war on the Ukraine. Chess is a war game between two players. No injuries or damage occur, opposing armies are represented by opposite coloured pieces. These can be sacrificed, for strategic gain without incurring injury or damage. The pieces are returned to their box, undamaged. Russia is renowned for chess expertise. Chess gambits are not suitable for real war.

Insurance

Travel Insurance

'Our contract will give you peace of mind,
we cover every contingency and claim;
a better one you'd be hard-pushed to find,
to give you satisfaction is our aim.'

> In Mexico, my son has just been robbed
> near the station... his situation's bad:
> by a group of five muggers he was mobbed,
> they beat him up, took everything he had.

'I'll send a form to him immediately.
FAX it back? No! A FAX is not the same,
he must return it, with the policy, to me;
without them, I can't process any claim.'

> 'He has no cash now, no clothes no passport,
> all his tickets and credit cards have gone,
> the Embassy is giving some support,
> so why don't you do more to help my son?'

'First, we must check his claim through carefully
and then, examine all the evidence;
we can't help yet, but in time, finally,
he might qualify - for some recompense.'

*I held my son's insurance papers at home; while he visited
Central America. Remembered talks between the Insurer and
us. His trip coincided with the Twin Towers attack in New York!
This delayed flights from North and Central America; prolonging
his stay and costing more (not covered by the policy). Months
later, recompense was paid for some costs from the mugging.*

Newspaper Reports

A fall from Favour

He had been the Don Juan of squirrels
before consuming hazelnuts in paste,
so popular with all the rodent belles,
his well-earned reputation gone to waste.

Now he can only hang his tail in shame:
no hopes of future conquests in the trees,
forest love-life would never be the same;
their figure-head had fallen to his knees!

*Based on a 2022 Press and Media release announcing a
new, special, cage-trap designed to hold hazel nut paste, as
bait for grey squirrels. This would contain an additive to
reduce the sexual urges of male squirrels: an agreed way to
control the births of grey squirrels, helping to regenerate
our falling community of red squirrels.*

Dress Code

She was still dressed in tasteful night attire,
when visiting her supermarket store;
she searched the shelves for goods she would require,
her slippers padding softly on the floor.

The Manager, who didn't like her gear,
informed her, discreetly, with a cough,
'Madam, pyjamas can't be worn in here'
so, then she took them off...

*A 2010 newspaper report, stated that a supermarket's
Management objected to customers shopping in their night
attire.*

Food for Thought

I wandered lonely as a cloud
Past shops with obsolescent tills,
Then as I bustled through the crowd,
I saw some bulbs of daffodils,
Mixed with onions sprouts and peas
And other veggies such as these.

Now when in quiet repose I lie,
Considering my favourite food,
They flash upon that inward eye
As something new that could be good;
And then my heart with pleasure fills,
And dreams of munching daffodils.

Based upon a 2015 newspaper article, reporting a forthcoming ban on 'the retail display of daffodil bulbs, together with eatable vegetables', (to avoid ill-effects on customers who might eat the bulbs by mistake).

A Wordsworth parody, (with his love of daffodils) how he might have responded before the ban.

The High Flier

She was proud – a Tory cow
Strutting with her head held high...
No contest, the bovine beast
Was awarded 'Best of Show.'

The beaming Judge, award in hand
Came forward to present and
Fix the rosette to her neck;
Disturbed, the winner hoofed the sand.

This was certainly her last
Haughty, cultural show;
The insult was too much to bear,
Her Prima Donna days were past

She was too conservative
To wear a **red** rosette
And snorted out aggressively
When she saw her boss arrive

Now the MP is much wiser,
For she scored a direct hit;
He sailed with elegance through the air
landing in the fertilizer.

A 2005 newspaper reported that despite receiving the presentation of a red rosette, a Tory frontbencher was happy that his cow had won first prize at Monmouth. The cow was less forgiving: on receiving her award, she hoofed her owner 15 feet through the air, into a pile of cow dung.

Faith & Belief

The Disciples at Pentecost

Who are these men, with vehement speech;
Voices emotional, and loud?
With gifted clarity, they preach
For every tongue, within the crowd,
Their message is of trust and love,
Faith in the man from Nazareth,
The earthly Son of God above...
A man unjustly put to death.

What is this message that they give?
'He died', they say, 'to save our souls
And have eternity, to live...
When God's bell of reckoning tolls.'
'Christ's death,' they say, 'was not the end...
He rose again and left the grave
To give us this good news to send:
"Each sinner who repents... He'll save!"'

Christianity – A hymn based on the New Testament account of Pentecost, remembering the inclusive teaching by the apostles following their meeting, after the Ascension of Christ.

The Youngest Sailor

She left her daughter, in a secret place,
To hide, and act as lookout for a time.
Back home she collected reeds to interlace
And waterproof them well, with mud and slime.

The mother, with a deadline she must meet,
Designed a special carry-cot to float;
Then, wrapped her baby son up in a sheet,
And launched him, soundly sleeping, in the boat.

A wealthy lady, with her retinue,
Arrived, as usual, for her morning bathe;
The currents quickly washed it into view,
A little object bobbing on a wave.

The precious basket gently dipped and shook,
The rich girl took the sandals from her feet
And, wading in to get a closer look,
Removed, with care, the folds of baby's sheet.

She plucked him from his damp but cosy nest.
Unwrapped and woken he began to cry,
Maternally, she clasped him to her breast
And gently wiped a teardrop from his eye.

Continued...

The Youngest Sailor continued…

'I can't abandon such a lovely child…
But if I keep him, what will Father say?'
She moved to put him down… and then he smiled…
! won't leave you to drown,' she said, 'No way!'

Deciding to adopt the little boy,
She named him from the place where he was found.
She'd have to find a nanny to employ,
And so, she sent her staff to look around.

The sister, on hearing this, was glad,
And from her chosen hiding place emerged,
She said 'I'll find a nursemaid for the lad;'
'Then do it now,' the would-be mother urged.

The real mother, brought from her home nearby,
Agreed to all the terms with willingness;
According to our Scriptures this is why…
She raised her son, as heir to the Princess.

Christianity: a modernised version of the Old Testament account of how the baby Moses was adopted.

The Road to Emmaus

Returning homeward:
despondent, all hope gone,
escaping the present -
two trudge the dusty road.

Deprived of leader, mentor, guide...
with shallow faith,
they recount strange events
to a stranger at their side.

The sorrow they feel
is lessened by his words;
their hopes renewed,
He joins them for a meal

and breaks the bread to share,
recognition comes too late;
when they realise who He is...
... He is no longer there.

Christianity: from the New Testament account of two departing, travelling disciples, who did not recognise their former leader: 'the risen Jesus', until it was too late.

Mixed Thinking

Spectral Analysis

'What are those colours in the sky, Mummy?'
'That's what we call a rainbow, dear.'
'What is it, what's it doing here,
why don't we get one every day, Mummy?'

'The bible tells us it's a sign from God,
that he won't flood the earth again;
we only see it after rain,
It's like a promise dear, a gift from God.'

***

'What is a rainbow, where's it from, Daddy?'
'Refracted light through raindrops, son;
they act like prisms to the sun.'
'What's a prism, what's refracted, Daddy?'

'A prism is a special shape, that's clear,
dividing up the waves of light,
Combined, they just appear as white;
"refracted" just means "split", I hope that's clear.'

'But how are 'colours' of the rainbow made?'
'Each wave has a different length,
each shade of light a different strength,
your eye and brain are where the colour's made.'

***

'See the red figures on this statement, son,
they're debits, cash I haven't got...
I need gold from that magic pot,
that's hidden - at the end of the rainbow, son.'

Doubt

Agnostic at Rest

Maybe some deity made me
as a plaything, just a toy;
this toy's worn out, its had its day,
the inner works no longer work,
the appearance, worn and grey,
no longer pleases any God...
It must be thrown away.

Priests proclaim: 'Heaven or Damnation,
for every soul departing...
leaving an empty shell behind.'
My Hell would be to watch the world
forever... without hope.

***

Through knowledge gained and passed along,
my contributions could live on;
but I can't share your future years,
we won't meet again.
I don't need shelter, food or wealth,
the crematorium burnt my hopes
and all my worries too.

Continued...

Agnostic at Rest continued...

Some may shed a passing tear,
but for me, the world has gone...
I'm in perpetual dreamless sleep,
without sorrow, joy or fear;
though winds may scatter me around,
opinions cannot move me now,
nor illness, politics and wars,
for I'm at peace.

The agnostic questions the human need to accept any one faith. most doctrines advocate peaceful co-existence. Strangely, more wars have been waged in the name of religion than from any other cause.

Attitudes

Floccinaucinihilipilification

You must have worked on this all night
Your presentation I can't fault,
The clarity with which you write
Is more than I could wish,
I must concede it's good to read,
It's lucid but it's rubbish.

Performance

Performance Poem

'A performance piece,' she said
gazing round the crowded room;
rustling paper and nervous gasps
are picked up by the mike.

Opened windows relieve the summer heat;
stifled coughs and restless feet
increase the ambient noise
and passing cars drowned out her clever speech.

Her written presentation had been sound

Show Business

The Casting Couch

As modest blush suffused her face
director said: 'you can't be shy,
I can save you from the dole;
you will be rich
this is your opportunity
to land a leading role.'

Outside the court, he hid his face
his lawyer said: 'you can't be shy,
I can save you from the law;
you may be rich,
but legal fees are very high -
today you'll end up poor.'

CCTV

Frank Bacon was a star of film and stage,
Included in the New Year's Honours List;
His off-beat acting had become the rage
In any part, by any dramatist.

His stardom brought him wealth as well as fame,
For any contract he could state his fee:
Such was the fascination of his name...
No dates within his calendar were free.

He read this public sign and was appalled:
'For crime prevention and security
Our hidden cameras have been installed'
He sued the Council... for lost royalty.

A Shakespearean Tragedy

No mewling mouthing ham is he,
unsurpassed and celebrated for his clarity,
his presentation can move the hardest man to tears,
a lady, of any age, would swoon with what she hears;
forthright, but renowned throughout the land -
here's an actor no critics ever panned.

Pragmatic and with no belief in superstition,
he blatantly ignores each thespian tradition;
by the footlights, glowing and magnificent, he stands
with arms outstretched and open hands;
then fearlessly proclaims that dreaded word: 'Macbeth!'
Alas, the safety curtain drops and crushes him to death.

Re-deployment

From sport and entertainment
celebrities are made,
based on past achievement;
for appearances they're paid.

Whatever expertise
helped them to make a name,
at home or overseas,
they'll bask in public fame.

When appearing on the screen,
to try out something new,
although they may seem keen,
they're embarrassing to view.

As 'presenters' they're miscast:
with hammed-up jollity,
their speech too loud and fast,
has no sincerity.

They'll use up every gimmick
with livelihood at stake,
in case their viewing public
cannot stay awake.

The Health Service

Dry Socket

My crown was off, beyond repair,
due to the tooth's decay;
so, I ended up in the dentist's chair
for extraction straightaway.

I woke at 4 a.m. in pain,
my mood **was** sour and black
I saw the dentist once again...
asked him to put it back

Arachnophobia

"There's a money spider," she said
"I hope it brings some luck to me."
"More likely to bring us germs instead"
He muttered, receding gingerly.

"I suppose you're right" she agreed,
"So perhaps we should set it free."
"Do it now before its microbes breed"
he advised her, scratching gingerly.

"Do you fear spiders?" she enquired
"Arachnophobia? Not me;
that's just a state of mind," he said
indignant, but squirming gingerly.

"Well, I am nervous, "she confessed
"Please, would you pick it up for me?"
"But then ... I might hurt it" he professed;
circumnavigating, gingerly.

"Look! On your shoulder-left a bit -
another!" She cried urgently,
"Then please remove it, SWAT IT! KILL IT!"
he screamed at her, shaking violently.

Earliest Memories

From 'Reception' he was led…
…directed where to go
at the lift he turned and said:
'I'd sooner walk you know.'

***

The lift stops at the thirteenth floor:
unconscious, there he's found!
and carried through the open door
before they bring him round.

'It's "Claustrophobia" you say,'
the doctor checks his screen,
'Do you have it every day?'
'Yes! All my life it's been …

… it started in my mother's womb:
amniotic fluid all about,
It seemed to me a damp and darkened tomb
I kicked and shoved, before they got me out!

delivery was quick, I'm told,
classed as 'premature'
escaping early had been bold:
prognosis still unsure:

"You cannot hold him yet" they'd say;
"Maybe a little later,"
So, while Mum waits, I'm crammed away:
inside an incubator.'

Stop

Invisible, lifeless, still passive;
aimlessly wafting:
a seed-like germ of death,
waiting,
waiting for a host.

No instinct, no self-drive;
carried by atmospheric flow,
through the air we breathe,
unwittingly inhaled...
... absorbed:
then growth!

Airborne, the regenerated, threat
builds and spreads across the globe
victimising the vulnerable and weak;
no cure is known
and protection may be breached.

Society is stricken:
close social contact's lost;
shortage of supplies,
handled goods unsafe

	Isolation,
Science struggles,	hygiene,
industry crumbles,	care
finance founders,	and patience
sickness and death	block it...
on the increase, day by day.	...so, they say.

The 2020 Coronavirus Pandemic; eventually controlled by vaccinations.

The Future

Welcome the Future

File away nostalgia
In the attic of your mind,
memories can be recalled,
while there's a stairway to the loft;
welcome the future, where new vistas lie,
beyond the confines of your living room.

The past should never hold you back,
don't shy away from change,
you can't decelerate your life
or travel in reverse,
look ahead and face the moving road;
keep a-pace with progress, motor on

Waiting

Waiting and watching,
the breeze whisps through my hair,
shuffling leaves nestle by my feet;
nearby, a leg-poised stray
dampens an indignant oak.

Waiting and listening,
a two-tone siren breaks
the grumble of the motorway;
now a clanking beer can
gusts crazily along the kerb.

Waiting, examining
each approaching car
for model, make and colour;

Continued…

> dark-tinted glass reflects,
> to hide the driver's face.

> Waiting, day-dreaming,
> minutes pass unnoticed;
> bad memories take over,
> nightmares of the past
> merge with events to come.

The Lollipop Man

The school stands half way up a hill,
facing a row of local shops;
a man, with uniform and pole,
patrols the 'zebra' to its gates.

Classes over, he's there again,
waiting to take the children back;
cars will stop when he lifts his hand,
as escort to our future world.

The Shopkeepers prepare themselves
For the invasion on their sweets;
prepared, the daily siege will come —
stampedes of little feet.

The trunk road leading to the hill,
is lined with 'Slow' and 'Thirty' signs,
to show a residential zone
and calm the traffic down.

The driver, in his souped-up car,
Imprudently ignoring these,
accelerates towards the brow
and crosses it... too fast...

Commerce and Technology

Analogue or Digital?

Salesmen will tell you 'Digital is best,
fidelity of analogue is poor.'
Why not ask them to put this to the test,
before you take your hi-fi through the door?

In some ways they're right, in others they're wrong!
to us, a track that's digital sounds great
and yet we're only hearing half the song:
encoded pulses, 'burnt' to solid state.

Distortion would affect the music's 'shape';
the modern way is: 'chop it into bits,
then save it to a drive (instead of tape)
where data from the digitiser sits.'

Persistence of the human ear is long,
those quasi-audio-scientists explain;
unless the speed and frequency are wrong,
those missing parts aren't noticed by the brain.

*Technology made it easier and cheaper to save and reproduce
sound, at the cost of purity. Tolerance relies on imperfect hearing.*

Reflections of a Scientist

If I leave nothing for posterity,
no éclat that leads to fame,
I won't care…
…in life, success could 'turn my head',
but celebration of my name;
will not arouse me, once I'm dead!

Continued…

Reflections of a Scientist continued...

History did not interest me,
or the feuds left in its wake;
forget violations of the past...
...ancient wrongs take too long to heal,
although we learn from past mistakes -
it is too late, to *'re-invent the wheel*!'

Geography lists the records
of many empires built and lost
too vast...
...learnt yesterday, now out of date;
progress comes at human cost
that's not repaid, however long we wait.

Science provides the nucleus;
an understanding of the age,
the basics...
...the foundation on which we build
ever-growing, useful knowledge;
at every stage an aim fulfilled.

The legacies of science?
Building blocks for modern progress.
The future?
Development is never sure
when each present-day success
may give a remedy too lethal for a cure.

Miscellaneous

The Animal Lover

He loved the birds, he loved the bees,
he loved all pets and wild life too;
a caring vet with expertise
and a practice, which quickly grew.

He couldn't bear to hurt a fly,
when stung by a wasp he spared its life,
animals in pain would make him cry;
but when at home… …he beat his wife.

Not any known Veterinary Surgeon; 'but you can't judge a book by its cover.'

Don't Confuse Me…

You're wrong, you're wrong, you're absolutely wrong,
I can't agree with anything you say…
I must admit, your reasoning is strong
and difficult to fault in any way;

the logic that you use I can't dispute,
the facts you quote are accurate and true,
despite the solid arguments you put,
I disagree entirely with your view.

Maybe a single-minded boss, MP or lawyer.

The Late Shift

"Last weekend I *were* working late,
in fact, I *were* on all night,
now fifteen quid's *me* hourly rate
wiv overtime *an'* such... *a' right*?

On Saturday the clocks went back,
that means I worked an extra hour,
me pay is short by fifteen quid,
It's no good you looking sour."

"From 8 p.m. to 8 a.m.
twelve hours are all we pay.
the clocks go on again next Spring:
arrange night-shift that Saturday."

Conforming

I'm neither large nor small
nor am I dark or light;
I'm gender neutral, a-political,
and neither dim nor bright.

I'm not at the peak of fitness, ---
neither am I weak
although I don't show prowess
I am not a freak.

I rarely suffer any strife
and never get too tense:
because I spend a perfect life,
just sitting on the fence.

Progress?

No longer responsive
to the garden's morning sounds;
I'm roused by early early light
seeping through closed lids.

The noise of cheerful birdsong
and leaf-scattering breezes
may break the stillness;
but to me all is quiet!

Oblivious
I finish a warm cup
and wind-blown scents compete
with the tannin on my tongue
I feel my aids carefully into place,
the silence is broken:
nature calls to me
through the open window.

My mood lightens briefly;
rumbling household appliances take over
then a chiding voice calls out-
advising of waiting chores ahead.

Hearing aids may not always be beneficial.

Excuses

Sorry! So sorry I'm late,
been held in a road-block since four;
they searched every car, for a man with a scar,
on all routes between here and Broadmoor:
the mad axe-man's at large... he's escaped!

Sorry! So sorry I'm late,
the water main's burst in my road;
engineers say they've been working all day
and the sewers have all overflowed:
I swam into town from my gate.

Sorry! So sorry I'm late,
vandals set fire to my home;
when Blue Watch came, they were fighting the flame
and my car got all covered in foam:
the fire-chief advised me to wait.
Sorry! So sorry I'm late,
our Club Captain was one player short;
with a tear in his eye, he begged me to stand by,
so, I played, in the interests of sport:
the match finished well after eight

and that is the reason, the reason I'm late

Prepared in advance for a poetry meeting, knowing that I would arrive late.

Blue Watch: *fire-fighting team in a TV series entitled 'London's Burning.'*

One of those Mornings

I was angry when I got up today:
it wasn't really that I'd overslept
and couldn't focus on the floor;
outside, the rain-filled sky was grey,
the forecasters had been inept
and life just seemed a bore.

My bread jammed in the toaster and got burnt,
the milk was sour and eggs were undercooked,
an unstamped letter had a fee to pay
(Something the sender should have learnt),
no papers - our house overlooked?
it was a dreadful day.

That unstamped letter had a cheque inside!
A nice surprise and quite a healthy sum;
my loving wife then rushed about:
fresh milk and eggs (now properly fried);
the doorbell rang, the paper-boy had come -
and then the sun came out.

Extemporising

An ill wind takes the speech you've just prepared,
you fail to catch and through the air it flies;
when you face the audience, don't be scared,
you can always improvise.

Late partying, you've missed the last bus home,
to come without a coat was most unwise;
raindrops! The prelude to a heavy storm:
be prepared to improvise.

You host a V.I.P. - forget the cost,
this pending contract you can't jeopardise;
you try to pay, then find your wallet's lost:
quickly, quickly - improvise.

A policeman is standing by your car,
waiting for some drunk, to breathalyse
and he's seen you staggering from the bar:
sober up and improvise.

While pruning the tallest tree, snip by snip,
step by step, higher from the ground you rise,
then suddenly, the ladder starts to slip:
now or never – improvise!

Hill House

I can still remember
The old house on the hill,
I didn't dare inside...
Played near it, for the thrill –
Those dark evenings of November.

Nobody lived in there,
Nor had for many years,
I didn't dare inside...
Those silly childish fears –
Strange feelings, difficult to share.

In the great storm that day,
Though getting soaked with rain,
I didn't dare inside...
Now no-one will again –
Struck by lightning, so they say

Hello Sonia

Sonia rang last night -
I didn't groan,
'It's two o'clock!'
I just turned on the light.

Then came all her news,
she didn't stop,
just rambled on...
I couldn't give my views.

'Passed my driving test
first time,' she said.
She didn't know
that I was not impressed
'Lab. results today'
came as a shock'
not my concern
she's in the family way.

'Meet me when you're free'
I didn't say
that she'd mis-dialled -
the call not meant for me

A wrong landline number, during the night; less likely now, with names and numbers stored together.

Wildlife

The Genteel Earth-Pig

The aardvark dines on special grub,
Turns up his nose at syllabub;
Endowed with a prehensile snout,
He seeks the best, when eating out…
The common worker he will snub.

He learnt his lifestyle as a cub,
No daytime visits to the pub,
But in the night, no-one about…
The aardvark dines.

Hidden under stone or shrub,
In open land or heavy scrub,
Torrential rain or in a drought

He never is in any doubt,
When visiting the Termite Club
The aardvark dines.

The Aardfox

The aardfox is a cunning beast
one you'll never see
not hidden in your local woods
or in the OED.

As soon as any cub is born
it quickly goes to earth,
mad scientists have tried in vain
to witness any birth.

Predators look high and low
in daytime and at night
but Summer, Autumn, Winter Spring
he's always out of sight

He has the perfect camouflage
adapts to any scene
you'll never find a scent or track
to tell you where he's been.

Now in my head, I really know
that creature must exist
but I need proof to tell me so,
I'm a mad scientist.

Lumbricidae

And as I turned the earth, I saw a worm
wriggling very quickly out of sight
into the clay-bound soil so dense and firm,
immediately reacting to the light.

Its soft segmented body tunnelled fast,
escaped immediate danger of the spade,
vanished (no clue, no trail of slime, no cast)
before it had a chance to be afraid.

Sightless, the only sense it has is 'feel',
a dark existence underneath the lawn,
the same old stuff to eat at every meal;
how deadly dull, the life to which it's born!

And yet, the creature doesn't give a damn
for bills, and debts, etiquette and laws,
it never has to sit for an exam,
or find the time to do the household chores.

No taxes, funerals or marriage vows;
no speed-cops, cameras or parking fines;
no need to surf the Internet or browse;
no hangovers from inferior wines.

Because it's physically bisexual
the worm's love life is second best to none;
in fact, it's doubly sensational,
one mate only, yet having twice the fun.

So do not denigrate the little worm;
although it may look ponderous and slow,
be jealous of it, as you watch it squirm,
it has a freedom you will never know.

CLIMATE

A Change of Scene

Thick curtains drawn back
the outlook dark, without promise,
bland buildings
line the deserted street.

A malodorous van,
with the promise
of Easter fare,
passes noisily through.

Fresh speckles relieve the greyness,
and float lazily groundward,
they settle briefly, then vanish:
the pavement glistens with the memory

Flakes multiply,
thousands land,
build: one upon another
hiding all below

A new tableau:
the sky clear,
homes are clothed in dazzling white,
on a crystal carpet,
sparkling in the sun.

A Climate Crisis

The towns fill up with eager tourist crowds,
with the dark season drawing to a close,
more sunlight filters through the drifting clouds
brightening homes and landscape as it grows.

The plant-life blessed by rainfall year by year
is parched and dry, since drought has followed drought;
once-welcome sunshine now is met with fear:
safety and future livelihood in doubt.

Warning signs are posted all around
some dangers may be lurking in the grass:
discarded items, thrown upon the ground,
mirrored lenses, from broken shards of glass.

The sun grows more intense, a deadly ray:
as heat builds up beyond the comfort zone
more grassland dries and moisture steams away:
draining scrub and bush, vital life-blood gone.

Unstoppable, the desiccation spreads,
a tinder-box just waiting to catch fire:
and now the outcome everybody dreads:
one tiny spark into a 'funeral pyre.'

Continued…

A Climate Crisis continued...

The bushfires spread to many miles around
wildlife and humans: all are under threat:
possessions and homes burning to the ground...
...no place to go for family or pet.

Advance evacuation's put in place
but some reluctant residents sit tight
(Ignoring all the dangers that they face)
they stay behind, regardless of their plight.

Evil smoke is drifting everywhere;
the use of special face-masks on the rise,
there's nothing left to breathe, but smog-filled air
from toxic fumes now carried by the skies.

Flames (fanned by gales at eighty miles per hour)
create two hundred blazing fires... ...and more,
intensity withstands all rain and shower:
wildlife driven out, frightened, burnt and raw.

The fire-fighters are local volunteers,
bravely working, to staunch the burning spread;
the aftermath will last for many years,
as lives re-build, while grieving for the dead.

The bushfires, started in the Adelaide hills of Australia in
2019 and continued until early 2020. A locally-based friend
advised and verified the facts of this terrible situation.

Acknowledgements

First, I would like to thank my wife Joanna for her understanding and tolerance over many years. She would leave me undisturbed, at the computer, for hours at a time. Also, she has accompanied and supported me at many, widespread poetry gatherings.

Thank you to Simon, Sally and your families for your tolerance and support over many years. Sally Paul and family together with their children, provided me with situations and reasons to keep on writing. Simon and Abi were very supportive during a particularly dark period, by organising professional CD recordings of fifty family-selected poems, read by two professional actors and myself; for presentation at my family–organised 80th birthday party.

Thank you to my 'big sister' Beryl and her daughter Valerie for their interest and support over the years. It was Beryl who urged me to get published.

A big thank you to Russell Thompson and Ann Vaughan-Williams and all members of Merton Poets and Whatley Writers for their friendly guidance and support over many years. It was Russell who coined the description 'recalcitrant' for my style of verse. Ann hosted special poetry workshops and also helped me with very valuable writing advice. We always kept in touch and it was Ann who introduced me to the 'Performance Poets' at Teddington.

A big thank you to Anne Warrington and Heather Moulson of the 'Performance Poets' for their continuing support and for involving me in their ongoing projects. Anne who very kindly wrote the Foreword for this book also introduced me to the 'Luther Road Poets', an offshoot of 'Performance Poets'. Thank you to members of this group for your friendly and helpful advice, which has helped me to continue writing, through some very difficult times.

Thank you to Father Philip Thrower, Father Clive Piggot and Ian Rutherford for your valuable support and appreciation of poetry written for the services and newsletters of St James Church Malden.

Finally, a great thank-you to my old schoolfriend John Yarwood (resident in Australia) who advised and corrected me on the true facts of the terrible 2019 bushfires.

Milton Keynes UK
Ingram Content Group UK Ltd.
UKHW041028070124
435586UK00001B/5

9 781803 816449